Monster
Machines

Written by Hannah Reed
Series Consultant: Linda Hoyt

T0359886

WorldWise
Content-based Learning

Contents

Introduction

Large machines are used in different places such as farms, mines and building sites. They are used to help grow crops, dig holes and lift heavy things.

People can use these machines to do huge amounts of work in a short time. Large machines are also used to move heavy loads of material over long distances. These machines are so big and strong that they can be called monster machines.

Chapter 1

Farming

Once, farms were small and work was done by hand. Farmers often needed to do a lot of work in a short time. Large areas of land needed to be dug up, and the seeds planted quickly.

Farmers used teams of workers, and they also used
horses or donkeys or cattle to help. Today, many farmers
use huge machines to get farmwork done. With these
machines, one person can do the work of many people.

5

Tractors

Big tractors pull machines that dig up the ground and make it ready for planting seeds. Tractors can also pull machines that spray plants to keep insects away.

Before tractors were invented, farmers used horses or cattle to help with the farmwork. Tractors have the power of up to 300 horses, so they can do a lot of work very quickly.

Harvesting machines

Giant machines **harvest** wheat, rice and other crops. These machines cut the tops off the plants and remove the seeds. They also clean the wheat or rice. They can harvest crops in a very short time.

Giant machines are also used to pick fruit because they can pick it much faster than people can.

A machine is used to pick grapes. The machine removes the grapes from the vine by shaking the vine to make the grapes fall off.

Find out more

What other monster machines do farmers use?

Chapter 2

Mining

Miners dig deep into the ground to find different types of **minerals** and metals. Miners can make **tunnels** under the ground, or they can remove the minerals and metals from large open mines.

Digging mines is difficult and dangerous work. Before mining machines were invented, people used **picks** and shovels. Digging even a small mine would take weeks of hard work.

Now, monster machines are used to dig mines. These machines can dig into hard rock, and they can remove huge amounts of dirt and rock quickly.

Mining machines

Miners use large, strong **drills** to make holes in the rock –
then, they blow the rock into smaller pieces.

Next, miners use giant machines called **dredgers** to
dig up the rock. After the rock is dug out of the mine,
dump trucks carry the large loads of heavy rock away.
The dump trucks have tyres that are taller than a person.

Did you know?

Mining trucks can be so big that the driver must climb a ladder to get into the truck.

Chapter 3

Building

Digging down

A lot of hard work needs to be done when tall buildings are built.

Before work on a new building can start, the land needs to be cleared. Sometimes, giant machines are used to knock down a building and take the rubble away.

Before the building starts, a deep hole is dug in the ground. Huge digging machines dig out the dirt and rock. They have big scoops that dig into the ground to take out the rubble.

Building up

Hundreds of tonnes of concrete and thousands of tonnes of steel are used to build tall buildings. All this material needs to be taken to the building site and put in the correct place. Many large machines are used to do this work.

Tall, strong cranes are used to build tall buildings. Cranes lift heavy loads of building materials. The cranes are put together near the top of the building. When the building is finished, the cranes are taken apart to remove them.

Building site / Keep out!

Chapter 4

Transportation

Freight trains

Some trains are used to move large loads of materials over long distances. These trains are called **freight** trains. Freight can be wheat, coal, steel and many other kinds of material. They can carry many different things at once.

Freight trains can take hundreds of tonnes of freight a very long way. But they can travel only where there are railway tracks.

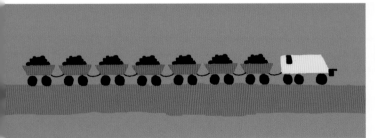

Did you know?

Freight trains can be more than a kilometre long. They have two or more engines to pull their heavy loads.

Road trains

Road trains are the longest trucks used anywhere in the world. They are trucks that pull many trailers behind them and are driven around outback Australia. Road trains are like freight trains, but they travel on roads, not railway tracks.

In some parts of Australia, towns are far away from each other, and there are no railway tracks. Road trains travel long distances on the roads, picking up and delivering **goods**. They move goods such as animals, mining materials and some foods.

Conclusion

Monster machines make it easier for people to farm, mine, build and move things. They can do a lot of heavy work that people cannot do, and they can do it quickly.

Glossary

dredgers machines with buckets that scoop up dirt and rocks

drills a machine with a pointed end that spins very quickly to make a hole in a hard surface

dump trucks trucks with a tray on the back that can be lifted to tip the load out

freight items that need to be transported from one place to another

goods things that are made to be sold

harvest cut and collect food from plants

minerals any substance that forms under the ground such as salt or petroleum

picks a tool with a long handle and a heavy steel bar at one end; the bar is pointed for digging

tunnels a passage that goes under the ground

Index